CARL WARNER

# A WORLD OF FOOD

ABRAMS BOOKS FOR YOUNG READERS
NEW YORK

If all the world were yellow,
A desert it would be
Of couscous, rice, and yellow beans
As far as you could see.

—⊣⊢—

Over pyramids of holey cheese
And golden grainy dunes,
We'd fly around in pasta ships
Beneath hot-air balloons.

—⊣⊢—

Here and there we'd stop and drink
From pools of lemonade
Among the pasta palm trees
In the mellow yellow shade.

If all the world were gray,
There wouldn't be much room—
For every inch of ground would sprout
A tasty gray mushroom.

Fairy rings and toadstool towers
Would climb toward the sky,
With long tall stems and rounded roofs
Like cities of fungi.

And where the land comes to an end
There lies a sea of gloop,
Where you can take a nice warm swim
In creamy mushroom soup!

If all the world were gold,
In autumn we would see
The golden leaves of dried cornflakes
That fall from every tree.

——H——

Around our feet so crisp and deep
This crunchy carpet lies,
Beneath a lamp of cinnamon sticks
And silent starry skies.

——H——

Drystone walls of roasted nuts
Surround our sweet homesteads,
Where candles glow from cobs of corn
On windowsills of bread.

If all the world were orange,
We'd live in pumpkin houses,
Where carrots, beans, and tangerines
Form trees and rocks around us.

—||—

Sunny streams of orange juice
Would tumble over peaches
And lap the shores of mango stones
On lazy lentil beaches.

—||—

Like glowing leaves, the apricots
Dry softly in the sun,
As beams of light warm gourds and squash
Until the day is done.

If all the world were brown,
We'd live on chocolate cake,
Where chocolate trains would ride around
A melted-toffee lake.

On rails and tracks of candy snacks
They'd clatter on their way,
Past chocolate-covered raisin rocks,
Where small sweet rabbits play.

With soft brown-sugar puffs of smoke
The engines would grow louder,
Bursting out of tunnels deep
From hills of cocoa powder.

If all the world were red,
The mountains would be meat,
Where rocky ribs of pork and beef
Cook slowly in the heat.

Upon a spiky jackfruit stone
A pepper scorpion sits
And stares across the salty plains
Of crispy bacon bits.

Behind his jalapeño claws
There hides a fiery sting.
His tangy, red-hot chili tail
Brings heat to everything.

If all the world were pink,
We'd live in a candy land,
In houses made from soft nougat
That breaks off in your hand.

—‖—

Licorice doors and window frames
And chocolate-button tiles
Would keep the rain of meringue clouds
From dampening our smiles.

—‖—

Around the house a garden grows
With jelly beans and gummy fruits.
And lollipop trees swirl round and round
On twirling trunks and raspberry roots.

If all the world were purple,
How lovely it would be
To live inside a garlic bulb
Beneath an allium tree.

—⊦⊦—

Snug within our scented cloves
Beside a riverbed,
We'd watch as flavored oil flows
From hills of garlic bread.

—⊦⊦—

And if we ever lost our way
Among the allium trees,
A garlic moon would guide us home
Through purple cabbage leaves.

If all the world were green,
We'd live in forests, fields, and woods,
Where curly kale and broccoli trees
Would be our streets and neighborhoods.

—||—

Like herbivores on forest floors,
We'd walk through fresh green herbs
And share our thyme with passersby
In leafy, lush suburbs.

—||—

We'd cross a bridge of cucumber
And climb upon a hill,
Then lay our heads in flowerbeds
Of parsley, sage, and dill.

If all the world were silver,
It would be made of fish,
Whose scaly skins of steely sheen
Would shimmer, shine, and swish.

—H—

Their heads and tails and ships with sails
Would fill up all the seas,
And waves of mackerel, cod, and bass
Would ripple on the breeze.

—H—

The early morning fishermen
On wakes of salmon ride
And balance on the salty scales
That rise upon the tide.

If all the world were white,
The land would be ice cream,
With trees and rocks so cold and sweet,
Like a frozen, frosty dream.

—‖—

Upon a misty mountaintop
Of fondant sugar frost,
An ice cream castle waits on high
For travelers who are lost.

—‖—

Within its tall white chocolate walls
Are rooms of every size.
And pointed towers of waffle cones
Rise up into the skies.

Instead, the world has many colors
and tastes from salty to sweet.
And with all this variety,
There's so much you can eat.

From yellow cheese and blueberries
To fresh green broccoli,
There are fields and farms of vegetables
And fruits in every tree.

So when you go to sleep tonight,
Make sure that you don't waste
The chance to dream of all the worlds
That you have yet to taste!

Desert - Couscous, rice, grains

Pyramids - Emmental cheese

Palm trees - Pasta

Rocks - Yellow peppers, lemons, yellow plums, pasta

Plants - Tortilla chips

Oasis - Lemonade, slices of lemon

Balloon and ropes - Ravioli, spaghetti with shallots and carrots

Gondola - Tagliatelle and crispy pancake, mushroom (anchors), beans (buffers)

Cargo - Mushrooms, cauliflower, tomatoes, peas, garlic, carrots, salami, asparagus, shallots

Pathways - Black-eyed peas, mung beans

Stones - Chestnut and button mushrooms

Bushes and trees - Buna-shimeji, enoki, eryngii, oyster, shiitake, and shiroshimeji mushrooms

Sea - Mushroom soup

Lamppost - Cinnamon sticks, hazelnut shell

Trees - Grape stalks, cereal flakes

Wall - Almonds, Brazil nuts, pecans, walnuts,
   cashews, hazelnuts, cereal clusters, shredded wheat

Windowsill - Foccacia, cheesy bread sticks

Candle and holder - Corn cob, bagel, pretzel

Houses - Pumpkins

Trees - Carrots, butternut squash

Leaves - Dried apricots

Rocks - Dried peaches, kumquats, tangerines,
   squashes, gourds

Stones and riverbank - Orange lentils, split peas,
   mangoes, chopped dried mango, cheese

River - Orange juice

Land and hills - Chocolate cake covered with chocolate powder

Tunnel entrance - Chocolate-covered caramel bar

Lake - Melted toffee

Trees - Chocolate cereal flakes

Rocks - Chocolate clusters, chocolate-covered raisins

Rabbit - Chocolate bunny

Train - Chocolate-covered Swiss roll, chocolate bars, chocolate-covered cookies

Tracks - Chocolate-covered crispy wafer bars, chocolate-covered honeycomb bars

Scorpion - Chilies, capsicums, Scotch bonnets

Boulder - Jackfruit

Desert - Paprika and chili powder, dried chilies, bacon bits

Desert plants - Lettuce

Mountain rocks - Rib eye steak, ox tail, beef ribs, pork ribs

Sky - Rib eye steak

Clouds - Meringues

Mountains - Pink chocolate

Landscape - Marshmallows

Trees - Lollipops

Garden - Marshmallows, gummy candies, sprinkles

Garden walls - Nougat

Pathway - Marshmallow (border stones), pink and white chocolate bars (paving stones)

Wishing well - Licorice candies, strawberry fruit strips, licorice

Cottage - Nougat (lower walls), strawberry fruit strips (upper walls), marshmallow twirls (upper walls), chocolate buttons (tiles), licorice (door)

Houses - Elephant garlic, purple Moldovan bulbs

Ground cover - Savoy cabbage, Greek basil

Trees - Garlic alliums

Stream and stones - Garlic-flavored olive oil, garlic cloves

Rocks and mountains - Garlic bread

Moon - Garlic clove

Trees - Broccoli, curly kale

Tree trunks - Cucumbers

Leaves - Thyme

Bushes - Kale, parsley, sage, dill

Plants - Green radishes

Bridge - Cucumber

Rocks - Bread

Waterfall and river - Mayonnaise

Trees - Thyme

Rocks - Lobsters, crabs, oysters, mussels,
    cockles, whelks, scallop shells

Bushes - Curly kale

Jetty - Razor clam shells, cinnamon sticks, olives

Islands - Cod, pollock

Fishing huts - Red peppers (walls), seaweed (roofs)

Telegraph poles - Asparagus

Fishing boats - Squash (hulls); snow peas and green
    beans (cabins); potatoes (windows); asparagus
    (masts); seaweed, peas, and asparagus heads (cargo)

Wakes of boats - Salmon, sprats

Sea - Sea bass, herring, mackerel, sprats, whitebait

Lighthouse - Zucchini

Mountains - White chocolate

Foreground hills - Fondant icing

Trees and rocks - Vanilla ice cream

Castle bushes  - Meringues

Castle walls - White chocolate bars

Castle gates - White chocolate-covered crispy
    wafer bars

Towers - White chocolate filled with vanilla ice cream

Roofs - Wafers and wafer cones

Snow - Icing sugar

Clouds - Bread

Mountains - Cheese

Trees and bushes - Parsley

Trees - Broccoli

Plants - Basil, thyme, parsley, purple sprouting broccoli

Rocks - Potatoes

Cart - Crackers, mushroom (wheel), red grapes,
    raspberries, blueberries

# To all children who love to play with their food

Cataloging-in-Publication Data has been applied for and may be obtained from the Library of Congress.

ISBN: 978-1-4197-0162-7

Text and illustrations copyright © 2012 Carl Warner

Book design by Meagan Bennett

Printed and bound in China
10 9 8 7 6 5 4 3

Abrams Books for Young Readers are available at special discounts when purchased in quantity for premiums and promotions as well as fundraising or educational use. Special editions can also be created to specification. For details, contact specialsales@abramsbooks.com or the address below.

## ABRAMS
THE ART OF BOOKS SINCE 1949

115 West 18th Street
New York, NY 10011
www.abramsbooks.com